is for

Blessing Magick

Kitchen Table Magick Series

by

G. Alan Joel

ISBN: 0988911299
ISBN-13: 978-0988911291

Email: ***alan@shamanschool.com***
Website: ***www.shamanschool.com***

Publisher: Esoteric School of Shamanism and Magic, Inc.

[this page intentionally left blank]

Blessing Magick Blessing

Child of Wonder
Child of Flame
Nourish My Spirit and
Protect My Aim.

This entire year be filled with the effects
of magically-sown seeds,
Thus, our lives be expanded by attitudes of experimentation
and magical deeds!
Upon the foundation of magical and shamanic practice may
we build,
Which keep us safe while carrying us through to what we
have willed!

The year past has been one of building force and
making positive life changes,
While this year present challenges us to renew our resolve,
choosing in all of life's
strangeness!
With the aid of the Winds, our Spirits, and Old Ones,
We work with our Totems and Intentions until done.

Honoring Magic's proper place,
In the Sixth World embraced by Wisdom and Grace.
Exploring the mystery and places of old,
Searching for the knowledge we seek to unfold.

To defining our aims and honing our skills we aspire
As we quickly succeed in manifesting what we desire.

Thus, my will, so mote it be!

[this page intentionally left blank]

Free Gift

To thank you for purchasing this book, I'd like to give you a

100% FREE GIFT

Learn more about your free magickal gift.

Access Your Free Gift at
www.shamanschool.com

Find a complete list of magickal resources on https://amzn.to/3swxvPo. These resources are constantly updated so check back often!

Kitchen Table Blessing Magick

Table of Contents

[this page intentionally left blank]

Introduction to Kitchen Table Blessing Magick

"We're asking you to trust in the Well-being. In optimism there is magic."
~Abraham

A Note About This Introduction

This book is one of a series of books in the Kitchen Table Magick series. Each book in the series addresses a specific area of magick (love, money, psychic development, etc.), and is written in a simple "recipe" format for people who want to use magick in their lives immediately. The Kitchen Table Magick series is akin to a Julia Childs recipe book, only these books contain magickal recipes for people to cook up some miraculous and magickal manifestations in their lives.

Because this series was designed so that each person could pick and choose to read just the books that pertain to their current life situation, each book is meant to be readable as a stand-alone book. To introduce the new reader to the series, this introduction to the series is repeated at the beginning of each book. If you have already read one or more books in this series, please feel free to jump ahead to the recipes that interest you. At the same time, some people feel that reviewing the introduction, as well as the "Rules and

Tips," is helpful before diving in. In magickal circles, your will is the guideline so choose whichever route best suits you... the Universe and magickal beings will follow!

What is Magick?

Many people have multiple different ideas about what magick is or can be. For the sake of clarity, here is what we know about magick after more than 35 years of study and practice. Magick is a precision science! It is also:

- The science of deliberate creation.
- The science of effective prayer.
- The science of manifesting Higher Will (substitute whatever Higher Force is most familiar to you) on the energetic and material planes.
- The science of heightened awareness, selective perception, and dynamic, harmonious relationships.
- The study of intention (as per Aleister Crowley, one of the greatest magickal practitioners in history).
- The system of creation, not coercion. Note: The word manipulation is often used in conjunction with magick, but manipulation simply means the use of the hands. It should be an "OK" word without a lot of charge, but currently it is used mostly to mean coercion. Look it up!
- The principle that every intentional act is a magickal act! Magic gives us the ability to communicate with beings on all levels, and allows us to understand, through direct experience, the actual workings of the Universe.
- The traditional path of spiritual growth.
- Not extraordinary knowledge. It is the "normal" way of life. We've just lost access to it. When you have this kind of knowledge in your understanding, you have the ability to resolve spiritual questions that otherwise become catechism. From a magickal point of view, catechism is not acceptable, since a practitioner must experience and verify everything for him or herself. It avoids the trap of dogma. In past times, having a

magickal foundation was essential so that we could talk directly to higher beings in the Universal hierarchy.

- Necessary to effective religious practice.

There is some confusion as to how to spell the word "magick." There are three different commonly used spellings: magick, magic, and majick. Eliphas Levi first used the form "magick" to differentiate religious or ceremonial from stage magick. All forms of spelling are acceptable in what this author teaches.

"I love Kitchen Table Magick! It's the best mix of both mystical and down-to-earth magick I have ever encountered. The fact that I can use items from my pantry is so handy and fun! It literally is about cooking up magic at my kitchen table, and having love show up in the least expected places!"

~Wendy J., Skokie, IL

Is Magick Real?

Yes. Magick is very real and has existed as a precise science for thousands of years. Whether you use the word magick or another name, this spiritual practice is very real. Every single person can learn to do magick. We are ALL born with the talents and abilities that empower us to do magick. The only reason that magick seems so, well, magickal is that this society no longer teaches the art and science of magick. In the distant past, magickal study was just as important as math, science, or the arts. In fact, magick was and still is the birthright of EVERY planetary citizen.

Can you learn to do the kind of magick portrayed in the movies? Yes... and no. The movies are great at giving you a taste of what you can do with magick, but they are not very accurate. In the Harry Potter movies, for instance, the characters use their Wands for every magickal operation. In reality, you can only use the Wand to handle Air energies. Your Wand would actually explode or catch fire if you tried to use it to throw Firebolts and Fireballs as the characters do in the movie.

So, what can you actually do with magick? Quite a lot. Here is a short list to get you started:

- Balance your energies for healing and manifestation
- Change old beliefs
- Defend yourself against physical and psychic attack
- Heal yourself and others
- Find hidden information and see possible futures (and change the future if you do not like the probable futures you divine)
- Psychically communicate with other beings
- Create sacred space
- Find lost people and objects
- Manifest what you want and need in life

At the very basis of magick is the understanding of the four elements: Air, Fire, Water, and Earth. Called elemental magick, these foundational elements are real. Air, Fire, Water and Earth are part of our natural everyday environment. What makes them magickal is the understanding of how they operate not just on the physical level, but also at the levels of Mind and Spirit.

For instance, while on the physical level, Air is just the stuff we breathe. On the magickal levels Air is the conduit of psychic communication, enlightenment, understanding, dreaming, and more. If you want more of these things in your life, then you need more magickal Air. How do you get more magickal Air? Wear more Air colors, including white for communication and sky blue for enlightenment and understanding. To take this one step further, you could also use various magickal techniques to take on more Air to make your body lighter. Take on enough Air and you'll be able to levitate.

By just extending your understanding and use of the basic ingredients of nature, you are doing magick! Seen in this light, magick isn't all smoke and mirrors, nor is it the result of Hollywood special effects. Magic is the result of truly understanding and working with the very elements that are all around you.

One final note: Many masters, including Wayne Dyer, have said, "You'll see it when you believe it." The same is true for magick. In other words, the suspension of disbelief and the willingness not to exercise contempt prior to investigation are requirements for magick to be "real." Magick is all around us, and always is, but our ability to perceive and use the forces of magick depends on our willingness to be open. No one else can show it to you, only your direct experience and observation can "prove" or demonstrate to you that magick is real.

[this page intentionally left blank]

What is Kitchen Table Magick?

Kitchen Table Magick is exactly what it sounds like—a series of simple recipes that you can literally "cook up" at your kitchen table using household ingredients from your own pantry and cupboard.

The Kitchen Table Magic books have been created for ordinary people who want to mix up a little magick in their lives without all the fancy rituals, but simply with everyday ingredients that can be found in the kitchen pantry, bathroom medicine cabinet, or even stuffed in the back of the junk drawer.

The goal of these books is to allow anyone with the desire to learn this craft to mix up magick literally at the kitchen table using simple recipes. What goes into a simple recipe?

- Everyday items as ingredients
- Easy to follow instructions that don't require years of training
- Procedures that take less than two hours from start to finish
- Built-in expertise that allows the magick to do the heavy lifting
- Some friendly advice on how you can help your magickal recipe provide the best results
- Oh, and a few little rules and guidelines about magickal practice in this specific arena that will keep you safe and sound, magickally speaking, when you use these recipes

Kitchen Table Magick Equals:
Quick – Effective – Safe – Everyday Use – Ordinary Affordable Ingredients

Why Use Kitchen Table Magic?

- Everyone can do magick.
- Magick should be simple, effective, and start working right away, else it is not magick.
- Not everyone has the time or resources to enroll in a school.
- People ask us for magickal help in hundreds of emails everyday... Kitchen Table Magick is designed to help these very people.
- Of the many areas of life, most people only seem to need help in one or two areas, so you need only buy those Kitchen Table Magick books that apply to your needs.
- Magic is for the masses, and should be accessible, affordable, and simple to do. This is what our teacher taught us, and this is the legacy we are paying forward as well.
- While there are many more advanced forms of magick, these books are an introduction to that world so that you can dabble, experiment, try things out, see the result, adjust and amend, and generally have fun... just as you would cooking a meal in your kitchen.
- This book is not for the major foodie, but is perfect for the person who needs magickal help right here, right now!

Who Should Use These Recipes?

- You and anyone you know who would like a little more magick and a little less ordinary reality in their lives.
- Anyone who needs help RIGHT now and doesn't have time to fly to India or Sedona to sit at the feet of a guru.

Anyone who does not have access to anything but a computer for help and guidance.
- Anyone who wants to do magick and then forget it (all while quietly watching the magick "do its thing").
- Anyone who wants affordable, down to earth magick they can do with regular ingredients in the comfort of home.

When to Use Kitchen Table Magic: Anytime…

- You need help.
- You don't want to do all the heavy lifting (leave that to the Angels, Spirit Guides, Animal Totems, and so forth).
- You seem stuck in a rut or corner with no way out.
- You've been struggling with a problem for a long time and need a resolution.
- You don't know what to do but you need to do SOMETHING.
- You'd like to learn how to practice the craft.
- You want to live a more magickal life and stop dealing with ordinary hassles all the time.

How Do We Know These Recipes Work?

- We teach a slew of these recipes in one-day workshops all over the country, via teleconference, and via videoconference. We also email them to people as part of our school's service work, or post them on our blogs and articles library.
- We have used them for over 35 years and still do, every single day – literally tested out at our own kitchen tables for over 35 years (and at thousands of kitchen tables around the world) for a quarter century or more.
- We receive all kinds of stories and testimonials from happy successful students.

Kitchen Table Blessing Magick at Work...

Read the following example to discover how Blessing Magick works in real life...

The Terrible Tenant Problem

I have been a landlord for well over a decade. I manage over a dozen properties, and most of the time management is fairly routine. I have a good rapport with my tenants, and we are generally able to "talk things out" when problems arise,

However, I have this one unit that is constantly inhabited by troublesome tenants. When one troublesome tenant vacates this unit, I find myself renting the unit to another tenant, who is equally troublesome, or worse!

One day I decided that "enough is enough"! The unit had recently been vacated and I decided to use a magickal house blessing that I learned in the Esoteric School courses. This involved using the materials that represented the four magickal elements (Air, Fire, Water, and Earth) to cleanse the space. I used a charged Firebowl with burning sage and resin for Air and Fire. For Water and Earth, I used a charged Chalice with spring water and sea salt. As I learned in the school courses, charging just programs the magickal tools with a purpose for the blessing—in my case, this meant charging the tools to clean out all of the negative vibrations that were attracting bad tenants

Following the process I learned, I used these magickal tools to cleanse every nook and cranny in the apartment, including the insides of closets and even in the crawl spaces.

Once I had finished my thorough cleansing, I held a few open houses (with fingers crossed that I would attract a solid tenant with whom I could develop good rapport). After going through my normal process for sorting applications, I chose a tenant, wondering if the house blessing would have a positive effect.

Boy have I been so pleasantly surprised at the results of that magickal house blessing! The tenant who moved in is happy, clean, and communicative. We have had a wonderful relationship over the past two years! I have now made it a standard practice to di a magickally blessing before I rent a vacant apartment unit. I have not had a single bit of trouble with a tenant since I've instituted this policy!

~ Billie V., Scotts Valley CA

[this page intentionally left blank]

A Few Rules and Tips About Kitchen Table Magick

As with any game, the game of life has its own set of rules. Specifically, the spiritual side of life has rules. Play by those rules and you will stay safe and easily attract what you want into your life. Break those rules and all types of unwanted consequences happen.

These "spiritual rules" are ones that have been observed, both in personal spiritual practice and spiritual practice with various associated groups and teachers. These rules universally govern any spiritual practice, and appear to be in effect whether you know them or not. Unlike ethics and morals, which change with culture and time, these spiritual rules appear to have remained the same throughout time, unchanging, like physical and scientific rules.

The rules in the following section are adapted from *Rules of the Road*, as created by George Dew, co-founder of the Church of Seven Arrows. There are two major rules, which are common to most spiritual practices, along with some minor rules that are specific to our form of magickal practice.

Two Major Rules

These two rules will probably sound familiar, as they appear in most major religions and spiritual practices, most probably because they are common-sense and apply not just to spiritual practice, but to life as well.

First Rule: Golden Rule or Law of Karma

This first rule is literally a "golden oldie":

What you do to the environment or to other beings in the environment brings similar effects back to you in your life.

Often recognized as the Golden Rule or the Law of Karma, this rule tops the list because it reminds all spiritual practitioners of potential unwanted "rebound" or side effects. As your spiritual power, focus, and abilities grow, this rule will have an ever-greater impact on your life unless you exercise caution. The Universe responds more strongly and powerfully to those with focus, power, and ability.

Note: As humanity moves further in the Aquarian Age, many spiritual practitioners have seen more effects from this rule occur faster. In the past, effects of this rule that often took lifetimes to manifest now occur in minutes, days, weeks, or months. In this particular time in Earth's history, karma seems to operate under a "pay as you go" system. Simply stated, expect the effects of the Law of Karma to occur quickly.

Second Rule: The Judgment of "Good and Bad" According to the Universe

This second rule adds clarity and detail to the first rule described previously:

If you are unsure whether your acts are "good or bad"—that is, whether those acts are in keeping with universal laws on this planet—the Universe will reflect its judgment back to you quickly, according to the "pay as you go" Law of Karma.

This law holds as true for individuals as it does for entire communities, states, nations, or other organized groups. If you are still unsure of the feedback you receive from the Universe, check areas such as your level of health, the soundness of social relationships, your prosperity or lack of, sufficiency of various needs in life, and even your "luck" with appliances and machines. If your luck appears to be consistently poor, then you are probably acting contrary to universal governing laws, regardless of your intentions. The Universe cares about what you do more than what you intend.

Additional Detailed Rules

The following rules offer more detailed standards by which to measure your acts or the acts of others to determine whether these acts are in accordance with universal laws.

- Do nothing that will harm another being unless you are willing to suffer similar or greater harm. What the Universe considers "harm" may be different than what you consider harm.
- Do not bind another being unless you are willing to be similarly bound. An example of binding someone is doing acts in attempt to coerce a specific other person to love you. There is no problem with attracting your soul mate into your life, but doing acts that attempt to coerce a specific other person to love you is a type of binding.
- Never use your spiritual abilities in vain, to show off, or to boost your pride. Using your spiritual abilities from a place of pride usually causes the Universe to bring instant backlash into your life.
- If you choose to charge money or barter for using your spiritual abilities in the service of others, avoid charging extremely high prices. Charge prices for using methods comparable to other professionals, such as an attorney or accountant.
- Never use any spiritual word, chant, litany, or similar "device" unless you are confident in your understanding of its methods, intents, and effects.
- When undertaking a major spiritual operation—one that will require significant effort or attempts to create a major effect in the world—use divination to determine whether you can safely benefit from such

an operation, and to discover the obstacles you must overcome. Divination methods such as pendulum readings, channeling, meditation, and question circles (to name a few) can reveal hidden factors of which you may be unaware.

- In any spiritual endeavor, take your time, think it through, and do it right!

The good news is that you can still cast a love spell and do love rituals. The ones we teach in this book won't get you in trouble with the Universe, yet will still allow you to attract the soul mate of your dreams. While you can't cast a spell to make a specific person fall for you, you can cast a spell to bring a partner of your dreams into your life (which may end up to be the same person, or be better than the person you've had your eye on).

The Ingredients of Blessing Magick

"Concentrate on counting your blessings and you'll have little time to count anything else."
~ Woodrow Kroll

Bestowing blessings on another is a great way to spread magick, positive energies, and to pay-it-forward. Blessing magick is just what it sounds like—any ritual that includes a blessing. For instance, in ritual we often bless people with Smoke from the Firebowl and Water from the Chalice with a blessing such as "For the peace of your mind, and for the joy of your heart." We also bless new homes and old objects to clean out junky energies and invite harmonious energies to enter. Blessing also invites higher beings (Angels and Totem Spirits and Spirit guides) into our lives to help us. Blessings given to another set the intention to receive blessings back on yourself.

Blessings And Gratitude Lead to a Higher Level of Being

Some scientists have studied the various parts of our physical body, such as blood pressure and heart rate, and found that people who are happier are also healthier. Studies also show that emotions such as gratitude, love, caring, and faith have a higher vibrational frequency than emotions such as sadness, depression, hatred, and fear. While this may seem self-evident, many of us don't make use of this knowledge. Counting our blessings on a daily basis opens the doorway for a positive energy flow, a higher level of being, and the consciousness to co-create with the Universe to manifest your desires. Recognizing this positive "blessing" energy is the first step. Sharing it and sending it out to others is the second. If you could raise every aspect of your life just by doing one kind act for a stranger each day, wouldn't it be worth it? This could be as simple as saying in your thoughts, "Bless you on your journey today", as you pass someone, or more complex such as paying double at the coffee bar and asking the extra to be applied to the bill for the next person ordering. Both of these are sharing your own blessings and that positive energy associated with it with others.

Blessing Magick Appetizer Recipes

Appetizers: Gaining and Sharing Blessings

The Blessing Way

Flower Essences

"I love the ability to mix up my owner flower essences to attract blessings into my life. I feel like these rituals are a cross between magick, creativity, and cooking up blessings!"
Ollie P., El Paso, TX

[this page intentionally left blank]

The Blessing Way

"When we give cheerfully and accept gratefully, everyone is blessed."

~ Maya Angelou

Time Required: Sixty Minutes

This ritual was used by the Navajo tribe when they were being moved from their native lands onto reservations, the Blessing Way or Beauty Way (in various forms) has actually been used in tribal traditions from very ancient times. It is an incredible magickal ritual that helps you connect with higher powers and beings and restores a state of inner peace and harmony. The part of the Blessing Way presented here is the Walking Litany which is a form of "magick spell work in action" that can be done without great effort but to great effect.

Ingredients

- Physical ability to walk the distance of at least two city blocks
- Being open to observing your own mental, emotional, physical, and spiritual conditions

Recipe Directions

1. Start by taking a look at your mental, emotional, physical, and spiritual conditions. This is necessary for you to compare results after performing the litany and note any changes created by it.

2. Walk for at least two city blocks. You can walk a further distance, but no less than two city blocks. It doesn't matter where you walk, as long as you walk the minimum distance. You could walk in a city, your neighborhood, a park, wooded trail, or even just around your house. Many people find it enjoyable to walk in a natural environment, but this isn't necessary.

3. As you walk, say this litany out loud and in rhythm with your footsteps. Use a strong voice of command.

4. The litany is:

   "With power around me, I walk in the world.
   With power within me, I walk in the world.
   This one carries power.
   This one walks in power."

5. Keep saying the litany over and over throughout your entire walk.

6. At the end of the walk, take time to again notice your mental, emotional, physical, and spiritual conditions. Ask yourself:

- What is different?
- What has changed?
- What is no longer present?
- What is new?

How to Use the Results of Your Recipe

When you do the Walking Litany, you are using a continuous spell that affects yourself. It puts up a temporary shield (magickally this is called an omnil) around you. Magickal effects from this type of shield can vary according to the words used. In the previous recipe the words would create the magickal effect of gaining personal power and/or ridding yourself of negative energies that are draining; thus, you become ready to recognize the blessings in your life. According to the Law of Attraction, when you are personally affected or changed, so is your life. In other words, “The level of your being attracts the level of your life”. The Walking Litany can help you change the level of your being, which in turn changes your life. The Walking Litany is good to use anytime you feel a need to regain personal power, create a more positive state for yourself, or create sacred space.

[this page intentionally left blank]

Flower Essences

"Every flower is a soul blossoming in nature."
~ Gerard De Nerval

Time Required: Sixty Minutes

Aromatherapy is useful almost anytime something is out of balance, especially in your physical body or in your emotional state. It is important to be in balance before performing many magickal procedures, especially blessing rituals. Many blessing rituals also include the use of flower essences or use the smoke from various dried plants as different plants lend different energies to the area. This recipe has instructions for how to take flower essences, followed by a list of various essences and what they are commonly used for.

Ingredients

- Flower essences that correspond to issue being worked on.
- One ounce dropper bottle.
- Spring water.
- Potable alcohol (such as brandy or vodka).

Recipe Directions

You can take single flower essences or you can mix them together. The effects are powerful either way. To make your own formula from tinctures purchased online or through a health food store. You can take single flower essences or you can mix them together. The effects are powerful either way. To make your own formula from tinctures purchased online or through a health food store, use the following directions:

1. Mix spring water with potable alcohol (such as brandy or vodka) in an ounce-sized dropper bottle.

2. Add four drops of each of the flower essences you have chosen into the mixture in the bottle.

3. With the lid screwed on tightly, firmly tap the bottom of the bottle against your palm at least 50 times to mix it all together (this is called "succussion").

4. You can now decide to either take the mixture from the dropper bottle three to four times a day, or add four drops of the mixture to a bottle of spring water to sip all day long (succuss the water bottle a few times if you use this method). You can also mix it with bathwater and soak in the water.

5. To decide the length of time you take flower essences, either take them until you notice relief in the issue or until you feel a shift inside yourself. Sometimes that shift will call for a switch to a different essence. Use

the following list of flower essences to choose a new group of flower essences after you feel a shift inside from your original formula.

6. The following is a list of flower essences for a wide array of issues, the issues that each can be helpful with, and the gift that each can provide:

   - **Water Violet**—grief, wanting to be left alone
     - ***Gift:*** *helps with tranquility, being at peace, bringing joy*
   - **Heather**—needing attention
     - ***Gift:*** *feeling vital, being selfless*
   - **Elm**—overwhelmed with present events
     - ***Gift:*** *helps one feel capable, responsible, and able to cope well with change*
   - **Olive**—exhaustion
     - ***Gift:*** *speeds good recovery, provides courage and dependability for the duration*
   - **Wild Oat**—boredom, not feeling useful
     - ***Gift:*** *brings forth talents, helps one feel useful, promotes definite character*
   - **Gorse**—hopelessness, giving up
     - ***Gift:*** *provides faith, hope, positivity*
   - **Red Chestnut**—worry, hypervigilance
     - ***Gift:*** *provides positivity and calmness*
   - **Rock Rose**—terror, panic
     - ***Gift:*** *creates positivity, calmness, courage, and strength of character*
   - **Oak**—overburdened, stressed
     - ***Gift:*** *supports one in being strong and dependable*
   - **Clematis**—short attention span and inability to focus, comatose state post-surgery, unconsciousness
     - ***Gift:*** *restores focus, alertness, and consciousness; especially good for post-operative conditions*

- **Wild Rose**—has lost the zeal to live, hormonal changes, pregnancy, adolescence
  - ***Gift:*** *offers joy, contentment, and acceptance*
- **Honeysuckle**—sulking, has given up, or feels exhausted
  - ***Gift:*** *replenishes energy and hope*
- **Mustard**—for those in deep depression
  - ***Gift:*** *promotes serene, joyful, stable, and peaceful states*
- **Willow**—unresolved resentment
  - ***Gift:*** *promotes optimism, responsibility, and acceptance*
- **Impatiens**—nervous, anxious
  - ***Gift:*** *helps with relaxation, sympathy, calmness, and diplomacy*
- **Hornbeam**—weariness
  - ***Gift:*** *brings forth certainty and lots of energy*
- **Red Chestnut**—incessant worry
  - ***Gift:*** *supports a calm and positive state*
- **Cherry Plum**—crazed, loss of control
  - ***Gift:*** *promotes calmness and returns a feeling of control*
- **Beech**—intolerance
  - ***Gift:*** *brings forth feelings of tolerance and acceptance*
- **Crab Apple**—cleansing.
  - ***Gift:*** *helps with cleansing toxins (emotional/ physical)*
- **Star of Bethlehem**—any kind of trauma or loss of a loved one, gives comfort
  - ***Gift:*** *comforts all traumas*

The following flower essences are especially useful for helping develop and enhance psychic abilities and communication with Spirit helpers:

- **Beach Plum**—helps refine and develop the

psychic senses in addition to the five physical senses; opens the senses to Angels and higher beings

- **Star Tulip**—puts us in more direct contact with Spirit Guides, while at the same time developing psychic abilities
- **Bayberry**—refines and increases the ability to hear psychically, also called clairaudience; increases the ability to hear messages from higher beings, as well as hearing the truth behind words
- **Caterpillar Plant**—brings one's own inherent psychic abilities down to a more accessible level where we can make use of them. We were born with most of these abilities, but most of them have been latent. This flower essence can call them forth for us to use.
- **Cyclamen**—helps one develop the psychic ability to channel; also useful for developing spoken or written channeled messages.
- **Jungle Flame Flower**—particularly helpful for developing clairvoyance, and integrating that psychic ability into one's everyday senses
- **Lobelia**—general tonic for psychic development
- **Marigold**—increases the ability to hear psychic messages, plus the general development of psychic abilities
- **Potato**—because the potato has many eyes, the essence made from its flower helps us see on many different levels and in many different dimensions as well; helps us understand psychic information and all the ways that information can be applied in our lives
- **Spikenard**—helps extend existing psychic abilities. The range of one's ability to hear, see, receive messages, or heal is increased when this essence is used.

- **Sugar Bowls**—helps open a direct connection to

psychic sources, information, and use of psychic abilities; also allows one to access new ideas, talents, and psychic skills

How to Use the Results of Your Recipe

You can buy flower essences instead of making them yourself, but be aware that without the blessing and active work of plant Devas, flower essences lack the necessary strength to be effective. They also lack the cooperative relationship between the plant and human kingdoms. It is best to use flower essences that are native to the flora of your region whenever possible; every region has its native plant Devas who know the intricacies and subtleties of balance for that environment.

Blessing Magick Main Course Recipes

Main Courses: Blessings for Blessed Sacred Space

Animal Totems

Four Element Circle

House Blessing

"I have used the House Blessing ritual for not only my house, but also for my office and other spaces I want to cleanse. It's truly amazing to feel the vibrational changes in the energy after I use this ritual."

Tony C., Redding, CA

[this page intentionally left blank]

Animal Totems

"Animals are not only beholders of great beauty, but they are also beholders of ancient wisdom."
~ Molly Friedenfeld

Time Required: Sixty Minutes

Using animals as Totems is a way for a person to become one with nature, to become spiritually connected with all of nature, and to show honor and respect for nature. Totem animals can bring us blessings through the guidance and insight they offer as we progress on our spiritual paths. There are also specific Animal Totems who specialize in carrying blessings. Offer them a blessing first, and then prepare to receive a blessing. In working with Animal Totems, you will find that sometimes they appear to you to give you a message or lend guidance with an issue that you may or may not be aware of. Sometimes you will call upon particular Animal Totems that offer specific types of help.

Many times, you will become aware of a particular animal showing up repeatedly in your life; this gives you an opportunity to study the characteristics of that animal and gain enlightenment into a situation that you are dealing with in your life.

Ingredients

- Ability to be aware of the animals that appear to you repeatedly in various ways
- Knowledge of characteristics of various animals and (or you can use the Medicine Cards and accompanying book by Jamie Sams and David Carson)
- Openness to watching for signs or messages from Animal Totems

Recipe Directions

You can take single flower essences or you can mix them together. The effects are powerful either way. To make your own formula from tinctures purchased online or through a health food store:

1. If you have an encounter with a particular animal in person, through pictures, media, or other sources, find out all you can about the characteristics of that Animal Totem. You can also look up the animal in the Medicine Cards book to decipher the message from that particular Animal Totem.

2. If you have a certain issue or situation for which you need help, think about the characteristics you would need to successfully resolve the situation Then do some research to find what animal or animals possess those characteristics. You can then call on those spirit guide animals for help.

3. Here is an example using the Owl animal totem: Speaking aloud or in your mind, say, "Spirit of Owl, I request your help."

4. Wait quietly for a few seconds until you "feel" the presence of Owl. If you are not familiar with working with spirit beings and are not sure if you feel the presence, go ahead to the next step since Owl always comes when requested.

5. Request help from the Spirit of Owl. For example, you might say, "Owl, please come with me today and show me what is causing my poor financial situation. Please show me this in a way that I can clearly understand. Thank you in advance for your help." Thanking Owl is very important (as with all other Spirit beings) as the Owl totem thrives on appreciation.

6. Now go about your day with an open mind as to what Owl will show you. Owl will ride on your shoulder, whispering in your ear, giving you knowledge and understanding where you previously had blindness and confusion. The messages may come in many different forms, such as a conversation between strangers that you happen to overhear, old memories appearing in your thoughts, a significant symbol or picture you come across on a sign or in a book, the words of a song, and many other ways. All you need to do is stay aware and open to any communications that come.

7. Once you get your messages from Owl and have received the information you are seeking, be sure to once again offer your appreciation and gratitude.

How to Use the Results of Your Recipe

You can also do one of the readings in the Medicine Cards book to discover your personal Animal Totems. Many

Native American traditions teach that each person has nine animals who act as guides for them throughout their time on Earth. These animals are connected to the abilities and talents the person has come into this lifetime with. They are also ones that will be needed to face challenges that will come about in this lifetime. These Totem animals come and go as needed, according to what issues we are facing at any given time. There is one animal for each of the seven directions that surround us—East, South, West, North, Above, Below, and Within. The other two animals are the ones that walk on either side of us throughout our time on Earth. Many traditions also believe there is one power animal that is with each person lending guidance throughout his or her life. This Totem animal is the main guardian Spirit for the person and the one that they can learn the most lessons from.

Four Element Circle

"Giving opens the way for receiving."
~ Florence Scovel Shinn

Time Required: Sixty Minutes

Use a Four Element Circle to request blessings from the four directions as well as Sky Above and Earth Below. This ritual helps you address the beings of the four directions with the blessing of being able to access their wisdom for help and guidance.

Ingredients

- A Sun Yellow candle that can easily be carried from place to place.
- Wooden or paper matches to light the candle.
- A pen.
- Notebook or paper.

- Compass (optional).
- A space 5-10 feet in diameter.

Recipe Directions

1. Locate the directions North, South, East and West. Use a compass if you need to ensure that you have the correct directions.

2. Create a circle of space about 5-10 feet in diameter.

3. Sit in the South side of your circle facing to the North with your Sun candle in front of you.

4. Light your candle with the wooden or paper matches, hold your hands above and around the flame of the candle. Charge the candle by saying the following verse in a voice of command:

   Child of Wonder
   Child of Flame
   Nourish My Spirit and
   Protect My Aim.

5. Now move to sit in the center of your circle facing to the East, taking your candle, pen, and paper with you

6. Write down the question for which you seek answers, clarity, or blessings. For example, you might write, "What blind spots do I have in regards to finances?" or "What is blocking the flow of money from coming to me?" or "I request help and blessings to get a job. What should I do?"

7. In the next three to five minutes sit quietly and allow the question to just sit in your mind. Do not try to answer the question or anticipate answers. Just sit quietly and wait.

8. Next, take your Sun Candle, paper, and pencil with you and move to the East perimeter of your circle. Sit facing the outside of your circle (facing East). Set your candle down in front of you and ask your question out loud to the East. Be prepared for a flurry of information to come at; the information often comes almost faster than you can write it all down.

9. Start writing all the information that you receive until the flow of information stops. Thank the Spirits of the East. Now stand up and walk in a clockwise direction to the next direction (South). Sit in the South and again face the outside of your circle (South).

10. Repeat the previous two steps in each direction, moving clockwise to each direction. In other words, you will start with East as described in the previous two steps, then proceed to repeat the process in the South, then the West, and then the North.

11. After you finish the process with North, return to sit in the center of the circle facing the East. Send thanks out all the way around the circle, thanking the Spirits of each direction, and blow out your Sun Candle.

How to Use the Results of Your Recipe

You receive different types of information from the various directions. This is because the beings in the different directions all specialize in certain areas. For example, the East will give you information about communication, planning, and ideas. The South will give you guidance on action steps to take, willpower, energy, and desire. From the West you will get feelings and Spirit guidance. The North will give you grounded and practical steps to take.

You can review your notes from the Four Element Circle immediately, or set your notes aside to read on another day. If some of the information does not make sense, you can repeat the Four Element Circle to seek further clarification; if you do repeat the circle, you may wish to word your question or request in a way that elicits more detailed information. You can repeat this process every day to channel power and force into your desired outcome—receiving specific information or blessings that will help you resolve your situation or problem. For some people, performing this operation every day gives them the feeling of doing something magickal, and helps them resist the urge to "do." Sometimes "doing" too much does not give the Universe enough room to step in and allow magick to flow into your life. When you are using a Four Element Circle, focus on letting go and trusting that the Universe is working its magick. Leave enough room in your life for the magick you requested to manifest in your life; remember that the Universe possesses far more power and knowledge than you, so allowing the Universe to act on your behalf is a great way to live a magickal life. You will find yourself pleasantly surprised at the results!

House Blessing

"May your troubles be less and your blessings be more, and nothing but happiness come through your door."
~ Irish Blessing

Time Required: Sixty Minutes

The House Blessing can also be called a Four Element Cleansing. It would be difficult to see your blessings or feel blessed if you are surrounded by negative energies. This ritual clears the junky and negative energies making your home a sacred space for you.

Ingredients

- A charged Firebowl, the magickal Fire tool (see the following section, "How to Use the Results of this Recipe," for instructions on how to make a Firebowl)
- Self-starting charcoal disks (available in stores selling religious or Wiccan supplies)

- Wooden or paper matches
- Pine resin
- Powdered sage
- Fine wood chips
- Sun Yellow candle
- A keyed Chalice, the magickal Water tool (see the following section, "How to Use the Results of this Recipe," for instructions on how to make and key a Chalice)
- Spring water
- Sea salt
- Water blue energy color source (anything colored water blue)

Recipe Directions

1. Charge (or program) your Firebowl for doing the house blessing (also called a four-element cleansing) using the following directions:
   - Sit in the South facing North with all of the ingredients for the Firebowl (Firebowl, charcoal disks, wooden or paper matches, pine resin, powdered sage, fine wood chips, and a Sun Yellow candle) in front of you. Light your Sun Yellow candle with a wooden or paper match.
   - Charge your Sun Candle by saying the following verse in a voice of command:

     Child of Wonder
     Child of Flame
     Nourish My Spirit and
     Protect My Aim.

   - Light another wooden or paper match from your candle flame and use this to light the charcoal disk. The disk will begin to spark within seconds. If the charcoal is old or damp, you may need to use metal tongs to hold it over the flame for several minutes, or light the top of it in the center of the bowl-shaped depression. Once the disk is lit, it will be very hot so avoid touching it with your hands! Place the charcoal disk in the center of your Firebowl, with the indented side facing up.

- Now place your dominant hand (the hand you use to point or write) near the candle flame. Pull Sun Yellow energy from your candle up through your hand and arm, and blow it out onto the disk. If you are unsure how to do this type of energy handling, simply imagine pulling in and blowing out the Sun Yellow energy. For beginners, imagination is the doorway to magickal acts of power.
- Place some wood shavings in the indented portion of the charcoal, then add the pine resin. Finally, place the powdered sage on top of the pine resin.
- Wait for combination of ingredients to burn long enough to produce a good column of smoke. Add more sage or resin if needed.
- Charge the Firebowl by saying the following charge verse in a voice of command:

"Fire and Air where you are cast,
Let no spell nor adverse purpose last,
Not in accord with me!
Cleanse these walls and cleanse this space,
Far from here send baneful trace!
Thus my will, so mote it be!"

2. Now take your charged Firebowl to the East most wall of the East most room in your house. Start on the lowest level of the house.

3. Draw a lemniscent (sideways figure 8 or infinity symbol) with the smoke at your starting location. The symbol should be drawn about chest-high on the wall. A lemniscent anchors the smoke to the wall.

4. Walk slowly along the wall letting the smoke of the Firebowl flow into the wall.

5. About every two feet use the Firebowl smoke to draw a lemniscent (sideways figure 8) on the wall. Also place a lemniscent on any windows, mirrors, or reflective glass/black glossy surfaces (such as TV or computer screens).

6. Continue walking along the walls in the house in an uninterrupted manner until you have gone completely around all the walls in your house and return to the exact same place you started. Once you have reached your starting point, draw another smoke lemniscent over the one you made when you started.

7. Put your Firebowl in a safe place (such as outside on a concrete porch or in your kitchen sink) especially if it is still burning for fire safety reasons. Now get your keyed Chalice.

8. Use the following instructions to charge the Chalice. Pour spring water into the Chalice until it is halfway full. and then add a pinch of sea salt to it. Swirl the mixture in the Chalice in a clockwise direction.

9. Take in Water Blue energy from your color source and blow water blue energy into the Chalice while swirling the water and salt mixture clockwise. Use the same method as when you pulled in and blew out Sun Yellow energy previously with the Firebowl. To charge the Chalice, say the following verse out loud while blowing Water Blue energy into the Chalice. Swirl the water clockwise after each line:

"Water and Earth where you are cast,

Let no spell nor adverse purpose last,
Not in accord with me.
Cleanse these walls and cleanse this space,
Far from here send baneful trace.
Thus my will, so mote it be."

10. Walk the same pattern along the walls again in the same way you did with the Firebowl, but this time with the charged Chalice. Dip your fingers into the salt water and spritz the water on the walls every two to three feet until you again return to the place you started. As with the Firebowl, pay special attention to all reflective surfaces. Spritz water from the Chalice on windows, mirrors, and TV/computer screens.

How to Use the Results of Your Recipe

If you are exposed to negative energies on a regular basis, you are most likely bringing those same energies into your home. You may need to do a house blessing periodically to keep your space clear and give yourself a sanctuary to escape the negativity.

How to Choose or Make a Firebowl:

When choosing a Firebowl, look for one that is made of brass, cast-iron, ceramic, or a hard hardwood (such as ironwood). It should be four to six inches in diameter, and four to five inches deep. It should also be a shape that is easily held with one or both hands, and light enough to carry in one hand if necessary. Make sure your Firebowl is of a shape that will be stable when placed on a flat surface. The shape of the bowl should also be curved-in and flared back out at the top rim to encourage the smoke from the Firebowl to form a thick column. Fill it with ground fire clay or clean, fine sand. Non-scented cat litter (which is ground clay) works well as long as it does not have chemicals or deodorants in it. Put one to two inches in the bottom of your Firebowl as an insulator to protect the Firebowl itself, your hands, and any surfaces from the heat.

How to Choose and Key a Chalice

Your magickal Chalice should be a goblet-shaped cup with a stem. preferably made of either glass or ceramic. Pick a Chalice that is either a Water Blue color or clear. Your Chalice should be smooth, but can have a light pattern. Keying your Chalice clears out any impure energies, personalizes it to you, and aligns the molecules for the energy to flow in a particular direction. There are more permanent ways to key the Chalice, but for doing a House Blessing, you can use the following instructions to perform a "quick key" of your Chalice:

- Cup your hands on either side of the bowl part of the Chalice.
- Locate a Water Blue color source.
- Begin circling Water Blue from your output (dominant) hand through the Chalice, into your input (non-dominant) hand, up your input arm, across your shoulders, down your output arm and out your output hand again.
- Circulate the color Water Blue for approximately three minutes, then stop flowing the Water Blue energy. Your Chalice is now keyed and ready for a House Blessing.

Blessing Magick Dessert Recipes

Desserts: Blessings for Others and the Blessing of "Enough"

Send Blessing Boxes

The Magick of Dayenu

"I never understood the power of blessings for me and others until I started using Blessing Boxes for others, and the concept of Dayenu (or appreciation of 'enough'). These two rituals are soooooo amazingly easy, and I use them every day to keep increasing the magick in my life. It really is true that a small change in the present, like doing the Blessing Rituals, creates larger changes in the future! My quality of life has improved so much, no matter the outer circumstances."

~ Steve M., Gary IN

[this page intentionally left blank]

Send Blessing Boxes

"Some wish blessings, others pray for them. Some send blessings and they become one."
~ Joyce C. Lock

Time Required: Thirty Minutes

You can send blessings to another person no matter how physically near or far away they are from you by using Air message boxes. An Air box is an energetic box filled with the magickal Air Element. You can choose from one of three Air Element colors (clear, white, or Sky Blue), which you create using the aura energy of your hands. For sending blessings, it is best to use the Air Element color of Powder or Sky Blue, which represents the spiritual level of Air.

Ingredients

- A color source for Powder or Sky Blue (could be a paper square that color)

- A location where you can use your hands to "form" an energetic box
- A short message of blessing
- A person you wish to send a blessing

Recipe Directions

1. First you will form an empty energetic box. Place your hands in the position to form the top and bottom of the box, palms facing each other. Start with your hands farther apart and then bring them towards each other, "pressing" the energy together.

2. Next use your hands to form the front and back of the box, again starting with your hands farther apart (with palms facing each other) and pressing the energy together.

3. Form the left and right sides of the box in the same manner and hold the box by the sides until you have filled it. You may need to practice making boxes until you can do top, bottom, and all sides fluidly without interruption in the movement.

4. Holding the box in front of your eyes and in line with the Sky Blue color source, pull the color into the box until the box is full. This is not a thinking process! Just pull the energy from the color source into the box – your intention does the work. The box is full when your hands grow warm or tingly – normally it takes no more than 5 to 15 seconds to fill a box.

5. You might also choose to send a blessing with Sun Yellow, even though this is a Fire element color, it is the color of life force. You can use a lit candle or other color source to fill the box with Sun Yellow, but never pull energy from the Sun itself since the Sun pushes energy at you and once you get the flow going you

can't stop it, which is very dangerous.

6. Envision the person's face in the box (or their full name if you don't know what they look like).
7. Put the blessing message you wish to send into the box either by seeing the words in the box (in electric white neon), or by speaking your message at the person's face in the box. Keep your message short.
8. Throw the box. Since it has been programmed with the person's name or face, it will automatically and instantly reach that person, even if you don't know where the person is, or he/she is halfway across the world. Distance doesn't matter where energy boxes are concerned.

How to Use the Results of Your Recipe

You can use Air boxes to send psychic or telepathic messages to people. Air is related to thinking and mind processes, so messages sent with Air boxes will insert themselves into the recipient's thought process. Sometimes, because the colors Sky Blue and Sun Yellow are "heard" primarily by Spirit rather than mind. If that is the case, the recipient's Spirit will most likely translate that message into a mental thought or even a physical action.

[this page intentionally left blank]

The Magick of Dayenu

"Remember that the happiest people are not those getting more, but those giving more."
~ Robin Sharma

Time Required: Fifteen Minutes

Take time to give thanks for the blessings that you already have. Roughly translated, Dayenu means "it would have been enough" or "it would have sufficed." This message opens the door to new blessings coming your way. People who are sincerely happy in spite of difficult situations are practicing the art of Dayenu. They look around at their world and say, "This is enough. This is good. We are happy." Or, to take Dayenu one step further, they say, "Not only is this enough, but the step before this would have been enough." Dayenu specifically says, "It would have been enough," not "it is enough." So the truly happy people who practice

Dayenu look at their lives and accomplishments and say, "It would have been enough, and we can be happy, even if we did not get as far as we are now ... even if we had stopped at the achievement or happy moment before this one."

Ingredients

- The ability to observe your own thoughts and beliefs
- The willingness to being open to looking at your life situation through a positive perspective
- A notebook or paper and pen (optional)

Recipe Directions

1. Take a look at your life situation. If it helps you to write things out so they become more tangible and concrete, then use a pen and paper.

2. Take stock of or write a list of all the positive things in your life.

3. Now look back at the step before each step on your “life ladder” and voice appreciation, gratitude, and your thanks for the blessings of how your life would have been if you had stopped at that step.

4. Continue this for as many situations and blessings as you can find in your own life.

How to Use the Results of Your Recipe

Here is a real-life example of using the art of Dayenu. I have two friends who continually amaze me—they are married, so maybe that has something to do with why they are so happy. Both were hit one year with acute and chronic physical problems, which not only caused them a lot of pain, but also prevented them from doing a lot of work and earning the same income they usually do. The following year, they recovered somewhat from their physical problems, although they still had many doctor visits and healthcare bills. But they were incredibly, oddly, amazingly happy. I asked them, “What makes you so happy? So much has happened to you." They reply, "Yes, it has ... good, bad, ugly, and back to good. Look at where we live. It's a chunk of Heaven! That's enough. Just having this place to live is enough.” Explaining further, they tell me that their physical problems have forced them to have down time, which they would never normally take. They have spent this time with their horses, enjoying their land, and NOT working. They used to live in a big city and had to pay big bucks to relax with the help of massages and therapists, and so on. Now, living in the country, they can relax for free. If they had nothing else but this land, they said, it would have been enough.

Do they have physical pain? Yes. Have they had to cut back on expenses? Yes. Do they still have bad days? Of course. But overall, they are living in the magick of Dayenu. On balance, they look for the happiness that comes from acceptance of current conditions, and appreciation of all that has come before that. They understand that even if nothing else good occurs in their life, all that has been in their life thus far “would have been enough.” This is the real definition of the word “Dayenu”. The beauty of Dayenu is that by living in appreciation of all that was good that has come before now, we always attract greater good into our future. Bumps in the road notwithstanding, appreciation of the past and acceptance of the present always (always!) leads to future good. It can be no other way.

[this page intentionally left blank]

More Magickal Resources

Kindle or Paperback on Amazon:

1. ***Witchcraft Spell Book Series:***
    - Learn How to Do Witchcraft Rituals and Spells with Your Bare Hands (Witchcraft Spell Books, Book 1)
    - Learn How to Do Witchcraft Rituals and Spells with Household Ingredients (Witchcraft Spell Books, Book 2)
    - Learn How to Do Witchcraft Rituals and Spells with Magical Tools (Witchcraft Spell Books, Book 3)
    - Witchcraft Spell Book: The Complete Guide of Witchcraft Rituals & Spells for Beginners (compilation of Books 1, 2 & 3)
2. ***Kitchen Table Magick Series***

Ebooks and Online Courses at ***www.shamanschool.com***

- Wand: Air Tool
- Athame: Fire Tool
- Chalice: Water Tool
- Plate: Earth Tool
- Magical Tool: Firebowl
- Psychic Development

- Energy Healing For Self and Others
- How to Do Voodoo
- Daily Rituals to Attract What You Want in Life

Find a complete list of magickal resources on https://amzn.to/3swxvPo. These resources are constantly updated so check back often!

Free Gift Offer

To thank you for purchasing this book, I'd like to give you a

100% FREE GIFT

Learn more about your free magickal gift.

Access Your Free Gift at
www.shamanschool.com

Find a complete list of magickal resources on https://amzn.to/3swxvPo. These resources are constantly updated so check back often!

About G. Alan Joel

Magick means many things to different people. The form of magick taught by G. Alan Joel for more than 30 years is steeped in tribal traditions from around the world, from both modern tribal cultures and those from the past, which have been mostly passed on through oral dialog.

At the very heart of the magick that Mr. Joel teaches is the use of Universal Laws for the benefit of self, others, and even the planet. These magickal traditions can take on many forms, including simple rituals for daily use, specific spells for particular life situations, the use of simulacra (often better known as voodoo), weather working, water witching, the use of the elemental tools (Firebowl, Wand, Athame, Chalice, and Plate), magickal self-defense rituals, and more. Also included are the use of the Tarot for divination and spellwork, divination rituals of all kinds, Spirit-to-Spirit communication, exercises for psychic development, and abundant healing techniques.

Through his 30 plus years of studying, teaching, and honing his magickal practice, G. Alan Joel has helped thousands of people successfully integrate the magickal, and seemingly miraculous, into their daily lives. In fact, one of the greatest gifts Mr. Joel has offered through his teachings is the ability for his students to always find a magickal solution for life situations that often seem impossible to solve. With magick, anything is possible in the mundane world. All that is required of the practitioner is an open mind, the desire to learn, and a willingness to pay some time and effort into his or her magickal practice. One of Mr. Joel's favorite quotes is:

"What you pay into your practice pays you back!"

While many magickal traditions have fiercely guarded their secrets from the public, Mr. Joel feels that "Magick is the birthright of every planetary citizen." As such he strives to offer magickal teachings that are easily learned and inexpensive (no excessive fees to join exclusive magickal groups or ascend up the levels of learning). He also offers techniques that are usable and effective for all who are sincere in their desire to practice magick. In essence, Mr. Joel's methods teach a form of "Every Man's (and Woman's) Magick." All are welcome, his teachings are simple yet effective, and he also offers online classes in which he helps students troubleshoot their magickal issues in an interactive setting.

Find out more about Mr. Joel's teachings here and on his website (***www.shamanschool.com***) where magickal offerings are updated on a regular basis.

Mr. Joel augments this magickal knowledge and teaching with 30 years of practice as Doctor of Chinese Medicine, including a deep understanding of herbology and acupuncture. His understanding of the healing arts deepens the magickal knowledge he teaches, as magickal healing is a major aspect of his teachings. Mr. Joel believes that while there is clearly a time and place for Western Medicine, magickal and Eastern healing techniques can be harmoniously blended in to offer people many choices for healing all types of health conditions.

About the Esoteric School of Shamanism and Magic

The Esoteric School of Shamanism and Magic was started from a desire for all people from all over the globe to be able to attend a real, if virtual, school dedicated to magick and shamanism. The aim of the Esoteric School of Shamanism and Magic is to help people create permanent, positive change in their lives through the study of esoteric magickal and shamanic knowledge. It doesn't matter what your esoteric background is, whether you started out with witchcraft, religious studies, spirituality or candle magick, we welcome you. We believe that the Truth is the same, no matter which form you practice. We delight in all manner of shamanic schools and traditions, magickal techniques and esoteric ritual. You can visit us at ***www.shamanschool.com***, our blog at ***http://shamanmagic.blogspot.com***, or on social media via links on our website.

[this page intentionally left blank]

[this page intentionally left blank]

[this page intentionally left blank]

[this page intentionally left blank]

www.ingramcontent.com/pod-product-compliance
Lightning Source LLC
LaVergne TN
LVHW052054160826
845678LV00015B/3213
* 9 7 8 0 9 8 8 9 1 1 2 9 1 *